From the Risale-i Nur Collection,
The Second Section of The Twenty-Ninth Letter of
The Letters

ON FASTING: Meanings and Messages from the Month of Ramadan

by Bediüzzaman Said Nursi

Translated from the Turkish by
Colin Turner

Published Independently

Also Available:

- THE SHORT WORDS: On the Meaning of
  Belief and the Value of Worship
- ON ILLNESS: Remedies for the Sick

April 2021

From the Risale-i Nur Collection

ON FASTING

Meanings and Messages from the Month of Ramadan

Bediüzzaman

Said Nursi

Translated by

Colin Turner

About the Book

The Creator says, 'Fasting is Mine'. And by fasting, here, we mean the wider practice of self-denial that is practised during Ramadan, when we deny our lower self – our *nafs* - the freedom to derive certain sensual pleasures wherever and whenever it desires. Fasting is loved by the Creator more than any other form of worship in Islam.

It is not difficult to understand why fasting is so precious to Him. Unlike the five-times-a-day prayer, the giving of charity and the pilgrimage to Mecca, fasting is an invisible act, a 'passive' worship, if you will. It is easy to make a show of your prayer, of your giving charity or of your pilgrimage to Mecca. This is because when we pray, or give *zakat*, or utter the *shahada*, or go to Hajj, we are actually doing something. And it is very easy to claim ownership over the things we do. But when we fast, when we fast, we are not actually *doing* anything at all. It is, for all intents and purposes, a 'non-action'. And it is practically impossible to make a show of our fasting because it is invisible to everyone but Him. Fasting offers the least opportunity for pride and arrogance. Fasting, then, is for God alone, and in it we actually have no 'active' part. This is why He loves fasting more than any other expression of worship.   This is why He says, 'Fasting is Mine'.

Fasting is unlike any other act of worship, in the same way that the Creator is unlike anything in existence.

Bediuzzaman Said Nursi's treatise on Ramadan is presented here in its new English translation. Said Nursi's main work – the *Risale-i Nur*, is currently being re-translated into English, with a focus on the communication of meaning rather than on strict, word-for-word equivalence, which often obscures what the author is trying to say and makes reading more of a task for the reader than a pleasure. We offer this as a Ramadan gift to all of those who wish to learn more about the wisdom behind the Ramadan fast.

Have a blessed Ramadan, and please pray for both the author and the translator. Wassalam!

Colin Turner
Durham, April 2020

ON FASTING

Meanings and Messages from the Month of Ramadan

In the name of God, the Merciful, the Compassionate

This treatise consists of nine points, each of which explains some of the instances of wisdom in the month ofRamadan.

> *It was the month of Ramadan in which the Qur'an was bestowed from on high as a guidance unto man and a self-evident proof of that guidance, and as the standard to discern true from false. (Qur'an, 2:185)*

The first point

The fast[1] of Ramadan is one of the five 'pillars' of

---

[1] Ramadan is usually described as the 'month of fasting', but Ramadan involves much more than abstaining from food and drink, which is what 'fasting' actually signifies. However, we have retained the words 'fast' and 'fasting' since they enjoy a currency that is universal. Muslim readers will be aware that during Ramadan, we abstain from much more than just food and drink. Non-Muslim readers unfamiliar with Ramadan may be surprised to hearthattherangeofthingsthatwearesupposed

Islam, and one of the faith's greatest signs or distinguishing features. There are numerous wise purposes in the Ramadan fast. These wisdoms pertain both to God's dominicality and to man's personal and social life. They are also linked to the training of the lower self known as *tazkiya*, and to the gratitude felt for all of the bounties given by God. One of the many wise purposes of fasting in Ramadan is as follows:

God almighty created the face of the earth in the form of a banquet table, covered with bounties, each of them coming *from whence he does not expect,* (Qur'an, 65:3). In arranging this banquet, God expresses the perfection of His lordship, as well as His mercy and compassion. Since we are enmeshed in a world of cause and effect, and veiled by forgetfulness, the reality of this situation is often lost on us. During the month of Ramadan, however, the people of belief suddenly take on the stance and demeanour of a well-organised army. As sunset approaches, they act as though they have been invited to the Pre-Eternal Monarch's feast, waiting patiently and worshipfully for the command, "Step forward and help

---

to abstain from is considerable. They should also bear in mind that wherever we use the words 'fast' and 'fasting' here, we mean the wider sense of 'abstinence' and 'abstaining' – i.e. abstaining from all negative actions - rather than just abstaining from food and drink.

yourselves!" The mercy of their Lord is compassionate and universal, and they respond to it with worship that is orderly, elevated and comprehensive. Do you think that those who do not worship in this way, and who are unwilling to participate in such a feast, deserve to be called human?

The second point

One of the many wise purposes behind fasting in Ramadan concerns humankind's thankfulness for God's bounties, and is as follows:

As explained in the *First Word*, a price must be paid for the food that the servants bring on trays from the royal kitchen. How foolish it would be, then, if we were to give the waiter a tip, while ignoring the one who sent them in the first place, and dismissing those priceless bounties as worthless?

God Almighty has scattered countless bounties across the face of the earth for mankind, and in return He requires us to pay for them with our gratitude. The apparent causes behind those bounties are nothing more than servants or tray-bearers. We are to an extent indebted to those servants and we pay them a price accordingly, showing them great respect and gratitude that in actual fact they do not merit. The true Bestower of Bounties is infinitely more deserving of thanks than are those causes, which are simply the means whereby those bounties are delivered. To thank Him, then, is to recognise that those bounties come from Him directly. To thank Him is to appreciate their worth and to acknowledge our own need for them.

Fasting in Ramadan is thus the key to true, sincere, comprehensive and universal gratitude. This is because at other times of the year, most people who are relatively well-off do not realise the value of the bounties they receive, since they do not experience real hunger or true need. Those whose stomachs are full – especially if they are rich – do not understand the bounty there is in a single piece of dry bread. When the time to break the fast arrives, however, a believer's taste buds testify that dry bread is one of God's most precious and valuable bounties. During Ramadan, everyone, from king to beggar, expresses a kind of gratitude through understanding the true worth of those bounties.

Moreover, since eating is forbidden during daylight hours, those who have fasted will say, "These bounties do not belong to me. I am not free to eat them, since they belong to another and have been given to us as gifts. I will therefore wait for His command." They will recognise the bounty *as* a bounty and they will give thanks accordingly. Fasting is in many respects like a key to gratitude, which is one of humankind's fundamental duties.

The third point

One of the wise purposes behind fasting in Ramadan concerns the social life of mankind, and is as follows:

Human beings have been created differently as far as the nature of their livelihoods is concerned. As a result of this difference, God Almighty asks the rich to help the poor. One way in which the rich are able to understand the pain and hunger of poverty is through fasting and self-denial in Ramadan. If there were no fasting, there would be many self-indulgent rich people who would be unable to understand how severe hunger and poverty can be, or how much in need of compassion the poor and the hungry actually are.

Compassion for other human beings is an essential part of true gratitude. One who practises self-denial in Ramadan will understand that whoever he is, there will always be someone poorer than he in some respect. Ramadan encourages him to be compassionate towards others. If he himself were not compelled to experience hunger, he would be unable to show compassion to others by giving them the assistance they need, and which he is obliged to give. And even if he were able to give assistance, without fasting in Ramadan he would not have experienced the state of hunger himself, and so his compassion would lack authenticity.

The fourth point

One of the wise purposes behind the practice of fasting in Ramadan concerns the training of the lower self known as *tazkiya*, and it is as follows:

The lower self – the *nafs al-ammāra* – wants to be free, and in actual fact considers itself completely independent. Its nature is such that it imagines it possesses the same kind of lordship that is ascribed to its Creator, and it reckons that it can do exactly as it pleases. It does not want to admit that it is being supported, sustained and trained at every moment through the innumerable bounties it receives. These feelings of ownership and autonomy are greater when the person involved is rich and powerful, and if that person is also neglectful, it becomes even more rapacious, gobbling up Divine bounties like an unjust, thieving beast.

One of the reasons we are asked to practise self-denial in Ramadan is so that everyone's lower self – whether we are rich or poor – may come to understand that it owns absolutely nothing, and that it is itself owned. Fasting in Ramadan teaches the lower self that unless there is a command from its true Owner, it is unable to complete even the simplest of tasks; it cannot even stretch out its hand towards water. The Ramadan fast thus shatters the lower self's imaginary ownership and lordship. Consequently, the lower self begins to worship and give thanks, as befits its true duty.

The fifth point

Another of the wise purposes of the Ramadan fast concerns the conduct of the lower self and the abandonment of rebellious habits, and it is as follows:

The human soul often forgets itself through neglect. It is unable to see its own absolute powerlessness, need and deficiency; in fact it cannot bear to see them. It does not consider itself weak and it refuses to admit that it is subject to transience or prone to disasters. It refuses to see that it is housed in a body that is nothing but flesh and bone, with death and decay its ultimate fate. Instead, it acts as though it possessed a body of steel, immune from death and decay. It attacks the world with voracious greed, with violent passion and endless desire. It is entranced by anything that gives it pleasure or offers it benefit. More importantly, it forgets the One who creates and sustains it with perfect compassion, and it pays no attention whatsoever to the outcomes of its life and its fate in the hereafter. It wallows in vice and it thrives on misconduct.

Fasting in the month of Ramadan goes some way to awakening even the most neglectful and obstinate of souls, alerting them to their weakness, their impotence and their need. When they are hungry, they think of their stomachs and they are able to understand their neediness. They realise how frail their bodies actually are, and they come to perceive how much they are in need of kindness and compassion.

The Ramadan fast gives the lower self an opportunity to abandon its Pharaonic tyranny. Through recognising its utter impotence and want, the lower soul nurtures a desire to take refuge at God's court. As long as negligence has not already destroyed its heart, the lower self prepares in Ramadan to knock at the door of Divine mercy with the hand of gratitude.

The sixth point

The most important episodes of Divine revelation took place during the month of Ramadan and so one of the many wise purposes behind the Ramadan fast pertains to the revelation of the All-Wise Quran. It is as follows:

Since the All-Wise Quran was revealed in the month of Ramadan, to ignore the demands of the lower soul by abstaining from food and drink means that we are able to respond to that heavenly address in the best possible way. Fasting, then, allows us to attain a state of holiness. It allows us to read and listen to the Quran as though it has just been revealed, or as though it is being revealed at this very moment, as we read it. It allows us to listen to the Quran as though we are hearing it from the lips of God's Noble Messenger (PBWH), or from the angel Gabriel, or, indeed, from the Pre-Eternal Speaker Himself. It allows us to act as the Quran's interpreter, to communicate it to others and, to some extent, to demonstrate through our actions the wisdom behind the Quran's revelation.

Indeed it is as though in Ramadan, the whole world of Islam is transformed into a mosque, a place of prostration. In every corner of that mosque, millions of those who have memorised the Quran cause the dwellers on earth to hear that heavenly message. Each Ramadan reflects in the most luminous way the verse, *It was the month of Ramadan in which the Quran was bestowed from on high.* It proves beyond all doubt that Ramadan is the month of the Quran. Some members of the vast congregation listen to the Quran reciters with respect, while others recite it for themselves.

To pander to the base desires of the lower self while situated in a sacred mosque, and to abandon the state of holiness through eating and drinking, is to invite the disgust of the rest of the congregation. Similarly, those who oppose this practice of fasting in the month of Ramadan call upon themselves the disgust of the whole world of Islam.

The seventh point

One of the many wise purposes behind the practice of fasting in Ramadan concerns the 'trade' in good deeds and the earning of spiritual profit, which is one of the reasons why humankind was placed on earth.

The reward for righteous actions in the month of Ramadan is a thousand times more than in other months of the year. According to a Prophetic Tradition, each word of the All-Wise Quran carries ten merits when recited, and will bear ten fruits in paradise. During Ramadan, however, each word yields not ten but a thousand fruits, and verses such as the Ayat al-Kursi (2:255) yield thousands of merits for each word. If they are recited on a Friday in Ramadan, the yield is even greater, and on the 'Night of Power', each word carries thirty thousand merits.

Indeed, the All-Wise Quran, each word of which

yields thirty thousand eternal fruits, is like a luminous 'tree of Tuba', which will earn in Ramadan countless millions of eternal fruits for those who believe. Consider, then, this sacred, eternal trade and the profits to be had from it. Consider it, and think of the infinite loss suffered by those who do not appreciate the true value of those words.

In one sense, then, the month of Ramadan is like a market designed for the trade of the hereafter. It is a vast tract of fertile land where the crops of the hereafter may be sown. For the growth and flourishing of actions, Ramadan is akin to the showers of spring. It is a brilliant holy festival at which mankind displays its worshipfulness in the face of the sovereignty of God's lordship. And it is because it is so, mankind has been ordered to practise fasting and self-denial. Mankind has been told to abstain rather than surrender to the animalistic desires of its lower self, its lusts and its desires for the trivial and the futile. By rising above its own animality and by ignoring the demands that the world makes of it, the lower self is able to approach an angelic state, and to engage with the trade of the hereafter. Through fasting, one approaches the state of the hereafter, the state of a spirit appearing in bodily form. In that state, each human being becomes a mirror, reflecting all of the names of the One whom all beings need, but Who is Himself above all needs.[2] Indeed, the month of Ramadan itself acquires a kind of permanence and eternity within this short life, within this brief, fleeting world. For a single Ramadan is able to produce fruits equal to a lifetime lasting eighty years. The fact that, according to the Quran, the 'Night of Power' is more auspicious than a thousand months – eighty-three years – is proof of this, if proof were needed.

For example, a monarch may declare that certain days of his reign – his accession to the throne, for example, or his official coronation - are to be public holidays. These holidays are designed to be a glittering and glorious expression of his sovereignty. On those days, he confers special favours on his subjects, appearing before them in person, bestowing on them honours and other bounties, and paying special attention to those of them who are especially loyal and worthy. Similarly, the All-Glorious Monarch is a Ruler, without beginning or end, of eighteen thousand worlds.[3] And the Ruler has revealed, in the month of Ramadan, the brilliant decree known as the All-Wise Quran, which pertains to each one of those worlds. Wisdom thus requires that Ramadan should be like

---

[2] This is a translation of the Divine name al-Samad, which means 'He whom all things need, but Who Himself needs nothing'.
[3] The iconic number 'eighteen thousand' simply means an uncountably large number.

a   special festival, a display of Divine lordship, a spiritual gathering for all beings. And since Ramadan is such a festival, God has ordered man to practise self-restraint, in order to draw him away to a certain extent from base and animalistic activities. The most excellent way of fasting is to make the human organs and senses, such as the eyes, ears, heart and thoughts, 'fast' along with the stomach. The most complete kind of fast occurs when we lead all of the senses and the appetites away from all unlawful things, all trivia and futility, so that we may guide them to the kind of worship that befits them. For example, the 'fasting' of the tongue means withdrawing from lying, from backbiting, from cursing and the use of obscene language, and to make it 'fast' from such activities. Once it has withdrawn from that which is unlawful, one should then busy it with activities such as recitation of the Quran, prayer, repetition of God's beautiful names, seeking God's blessings on the Prophet, and asking for forgiveness.

The eyes, too, should 'fast' by abstaining from that which is unlawful, such as looking at members of the opposite sex who are outside the circle of kinship[4], or indeed at anything that is unlawful. And they should be used instead to look at that which is lawful and

---

4 One's 'circle of kinship' signifies those members of the extended family that one is not allowed to marry.

learn from it. Similarly, the ears should 'fast' by refusing to listen to that which is harmful, and should be employed instead to listen to the Quran, and so on. Indeed all of one's organs and senses should 'fast'. And this should not be that difficult, for once the stomach – which is the body's largest and most complex factory – has been forced to take a holiday from work through fasting, it should be relatively easy to make the smaller 'workshops' in the body follow suit.

The eighth point

Another of the wise purposes behind the Ramadan fast concerns man's personal life, and is as follows:

The Ramadan fast from food and drink is a healing physical and spiritual programme of the most important kind. When one's lower soul leads one to eat and drink as one pleases, it is not only harmful for us physically, from a medical point of view. For when we fall on things and devour them like vultures, without considering whether they are lawful or unlawful, we poison our spiritual life as well. Such a soul finds it very difficult to obey the heart or the spirit.[5] It is more than happy to take the reins in its own hands,

---

[5] The soul (*nafs*) should of course be distinguished from the spirit (*rūḥ*), even though some tend to conflate the two. (Translator)

and gradually turns into something utterly uncontrollable. Instead of being mounted and led by its owner, the lower self turns into a beast that mounts its owner and rides him or her wherever its fancy takes it. Fasting in Ramadan, however, and the fast from food and drink in particular, trains the lower self and makes it accustomed to a kind of diet. Gradually, the soul begins to discipline itself and learns to listen to, and obey, commands.

Furthermore, through fasting, the lower self will no longer be making the wretched stomach ill by stuffing it full of food before the last meal has even been digested. And by withdrawing even from lawful acts, as it is ordered to do, the soul will learn how to listen to the commands of both the Sharia and human reason, and thus avoid that which is unlawful. In short, it will try not to destroy its owner's spiritual life.

Furthermore, the vast majority of human beings often suffer from hunger. Human beings thus need both hunger and discipline in order to be able to learn patience and endurance. Fasting in Ramadan means the patient endurance of a period of hunger that is longer than fifteen hours in most places. As such, it provides discipline and is a kind of prolonged training session. Fasting, if done properly, is certainly a cure for impatience and lack of endurance, both of which tend to prolong or increase man's affliction.

Furthermore, the stomach is like a factory with numerous workers, and many of the body's organs are connected to it. If the lower self does take a rest during this month, it makes the factory's workers and the organs attached to it forget their particular duties. It keeps them so busy that they remain imprisoned under its tyranny. They become so confused and distracted by the continuous hustle and bustle of the factory that all of the workers, and all of the other organs, cannot help but forget their real and most valuable duties. It is for this reason that for centuries, those close to God have disciplined themselves through fasting in order to train their souls and attain perfection. Through fasting in Ramadan, the factory's workers understand that they were not created solely for the sake of the factory. Similarly, the rest of the organs are freed from the base amusements of the factory and are able to delight in the more elevated pleasures of the spirit. It is for this reason that in Ramadan, the believers experience forms of enlightenment and spiritual joy which differ in accordance with their degrees. Consequently the subtle faculties - such as the heart, the intellect and the spirit - make great progress during Ramadan on account of the fasting and self-denial. The stomach may indeed weep, but the rest of the organs, limbs, and senses jump for joy.

The ninth point

One of the wise purposes behind the fast of Ramadan pertains to the shattering of the lower self's imaginary ownership and sense of lordship, and to the exposure of its impotence, which is necessary if it is to realise that its duty is one of worship.

The lower self does not want to recognise the One Who sustains it. Instead, it wishes to express its own lordship, just as Pharaoh did. Its character remains the same, regardless of how much torment it puts itself through in its quest for self-worship. There is one thing, however, which is able to bring it to its knees, and that is hunger. Therefore the Ramadan practice of self-denial in general, and the fast in particular, strikes direct blows at the heart of the lower self's Pharaoh-like façade, shattering it completely. The fast exposes the self's impotence, its weakness and its need. In short, it makes it realise that it is a slave.

Among the Prophetic Traditions is the following:

> God Almighty said to the lower self, 'What am I and what are you?' The lower self replied, 'I am myself and You are Yourself.' So God punished it and cast it into hell. Then He asked

it again, 'What am I and what are you?' And again it replied, 'I am myself and You are Yourself.' However much God punished it, still it would not relinquish its egoism. Finally, God punished it with hunger. Then, when he asked it, 'What am I and what are you?', the self replied, 'You are my Compassionate Sustainer and I am your impotent slave.'

O God! Grant blessings and peace to our master Muhammad, that will be pleasing to You and fulfilment of his truth to the number of the merits of the words of the Qur'an in the month of Ramadan, and to his Family and Companions, and grant them peace.

*Limitless in His glory is your Sustainer, the Lord of Almightiness, [exalted] above anything that men may devise by way of definition! * And peace be upon all His message-bearers. * And all praise is due to God alone, the Sustainer of All the Worlds!*

The Life and Thought of

BEDIUZZAMAN SAID NURSI

The Life and Thought of
BEDIUZZAMAN SAID NURSI

Said Nursi (1878-1960) is a contemporary scholar and thinker who is best known for his monumental work, the *Risale-i Nur (Epistles of Light)*, a six-thousand page thematic commentary on the Quran. Born in Nurs, a tiny village in the province of Bitlis in eastern Turkey, Nursi spent his early and adolescent years studying the classical Islamic curriculum in various traditional madrasas in the area. He was an exceptionally gifted student who excelled in his studies to the extent that he was able to receive his 'finishing diploma' in 1892 at the tender age of fourteen. Later when he went to Van, a province in eastern Turkey, he also studied the natural sciences in the library of Tahir Pasha, governor of the province. By this point, Nursi was so renowned for his intellectual and academic acumen that he had been given the epithet 'Bediuzzaman' (Wonder of the Age).

Nursi realized that one of the shortcomings of the traditional madrasa education was its omission of the modern sciences, which meant that madrasa students were not able to establish harmony between these new sciences and the traditional disciplines. And so it became his ambition, even at this very young age, to establish a university where the modern sciences could be studied alongside the traditional, Islamic disciplines. When the Ottoman Empire collapsed and the Turkish Republic was established in 1923, Nursi was invited to Ankara, where a role in the new government was offered to him. However, he realised that given the turbulent circumstances there, it would not be possible to carry out his original plan. He decided at this point to withdraw from all engagement with politics. He returned to Van in the spring of 1923, referring to himself now as the 'New Said'.

Nursi found that his life was being shaken at this time by the fast-growing current of aggressive secularism that was sweeping the county, and so during this period of his life, Nursi spent most of his time with his students quietly on Mount Erek, where he passed all of his private time in prayer and contemplation. In February 1925, however, his pastoral idyll was shaken by the Kurdish revolt – an insurrection which Nursi had warned everyone not to join and not to support. Despite his warnings, however, Nursi was implicated as a participant in the revolt and he was sent into exile as a result. This exile set an unfortunate precedent, for most of the rest of Bediuzzaman's life would be spent either in exile or in prison.

Following his exile to Burdur, Nursi was exiled to Barla, a village in the province of Isparta, where he lived under house arrest from March 1927 until July 1934. Most of the treatises that comprise the *Risale-i Nur* were written during these comparatively peaceful years in Barla. Along with his students, Nursi was brought to Eskişehir to stand trial, a process which began in May 1935 and lasted almost a year. The standard charge levelled against Nursi and his students, and indeed against anyone who read and defended the Qur'an at this time, was that of "violating secularism". Prison conditions at that time were horrendous, and Nursi tried to encourage his students to think of their incarceration as a kind of school, one which he called 'The School of Joseph' (*Medrese-i Yûsufiye*), in memory of the Prophet Joseph, who had also been imprisoned unjustly, and who taught his fellow prisoners, leading them to belief in God. When Nursi was released he was sent to Kastamonu, where he was detained under house arrest from March 1936 until September 1943.

A significant change took place in May 1950 when the newly formed Democratic Party came to power. The new government was sympathetic towards religion and so Bediuzzaman was able to enjoy a certain amount of freedom, albeit still with a number of restrictions. The last ten years of his life was referred to by Nursi himself as the period of the 'Third Said' (September 1949–23 March 1960). The general amnesty of 14 July 1950 brought with it a relative freedom and so he decided to settle in Isparta, where he kept with him a small number of young students to assist him and to be trained. He referred to these years as the 'Third Said' years, when he continued to devote much of his time to issues related to the *Risale-i Nur*. He instituted the practice of communal reading (*ders*) of the *Risale-i Nur* that would later become the central activity of the Nur community, and each day would hold readings with the students who resided with him. But by the turn of the decade his health was failing. On 20th March 1960 he set off with three of his students for Urfa in south- east Turkey, where on the 23rd March he died.

Nursi was a passionate advocate of personal rights and freedoms, as exemplified by his saying "I can live without bread, but not without freedom." He objected to any association of Islam with oppression and tyranny, stating that Islam came to this world to end injustice and despotism. He defined despotism as "... the basis of tyranny. It annihilates humanity. It is despotism which reduces man to the most abject valleys of abasement, causing the Islamic world to sink into abjection and degradation, arousing animosity and malice, poisoning Islam... and causing endless conflict among Muslims."

Unlike many of his contemporaries who associated Islam with politics, Nursi abstained from mixing religion with politics and remained distant from the notion of 'political Islam.' Instead, he focused on personal dimension of belief and religion, stating that saving the faith of even a single person is of the utmost importance. Despite all the injustices and harassment to which he was subjected, he lived by the principle of 'positive action' always, never advocating violence. He stressed repeatedly that Muslims must now in this age of enlightenment and civilization fight wars with the pen and not the sword. Moreover, he viewed aggressive atheism as the greatest threat to humanity, stating that Muslims and pious Christians must join forces to overcome this threat, which endangers the eternal life of the whole of humanity.

The hallmark of Nursi's teachings is his emphasis on belief – belief in God and belief in the hereafter, which are tenets shared by all of the Abrahamic faiths. After the formation of the new Turkish Republic in the 1920s and the imposition of aggressive secular policies, Nursi devoted himself to saving and strengthening belief in God and the other principles of faith that were at that time coming under attack. He argues that death is a new beginning and is "... not execution, or nothingness, or annihilation; it is not cessation, or extinction; it is not eternal separation, or non-existence, or a random event, or an authorless obliteration. Rather, it is a discharge from duty given by the One Who is All-Wise and All-Compassionate; it is a change of locations. It is a dispatch to eternal bliss, to your true home." For Nursi, attaining strong belief is like gaining an eternal world. Therefore, these two articles of faith are the foundation of human identity that gives humankind a responsibility in this world to be God's vicegerent on Earth in order to preserve order and prevent corruption (see the Qur'an, 2: 30f).

Nursi points out that human beings have desires and hopes that stretch to eternity, thoughts and imaginings that embrace the whole universe, together with an earnest desire for everlasting happiness and Paradise, and various innate capacities and abilities on which no limit has been placed. People are exposed to attacks from innumerable enemies and to blows from innumerable calamities, despite their countless needs, their weakness and their impotence. Under the constant threat of death, they live out their brief and turbulent lives in mostly wretched circumstances. Nursi believed that the main mission of humankind is "to progress through the acquisition of knowledge", that is, "to aim at reaching perfection via knowledge". But the highest aim of knowledge, and the thing which makes it valuable, is the knowledge of God (*ma'rifatullah*).

No matter what we say about scholars it is always best for them to speak for themselves. We thus leave you with this short work here and ask that you judge the tree by its fruit. For further reading we can recommend the following works about Bediuzzaman Said Nursi's life and ideas: Colin Turner, *The Qur'an Revealed: A Critical Analysis of Said Nursi's Epistles of Light*, Berlin: Gerlach Press, 2013; Şükran Vahide and Ibrahim M Abu-Rabi'. *Islam in Modern Turkey: An Intellectual Biography of Bediuzzaman Said Nursi*, Albany: State University of New York Press, 2008.

Nursi Society Editorial Board

www.ingramcontent.com/pod-product-compliance
Lightning Source LLC
Chambersburg PA
CBHW070818170726
48000CB00018B/1384